To Jeff
Keep on steaming!

Rob Wheatley

Bruce Wheatley

Rails over the Great Divide. 3820, Brewongle – January 1974.

Railway Portraits

ROBERT & BRUCE WHEATLEY

Foreword by Clive Robertson

Loco Inspector Stewart Bates and Philip Fowler. 3827, Yass – January 1970.

Published in 2006 by WriteLight Pty Ltd
for Robert and Bruce Wheatley.
Tel: (02) 4757 3570.
Email: railwayportraits@aapt.net.au
Website: www.railwayportraits.com.au

© text and photographs Robert & Bruce Wheatley

Production by Victoria Jefferys. Design & layout by Julianne Billington.
Printed in China through Phoenix Offset.

Reprinted 2008, 2009, 2010

National Library of Australia Cataloguing-in-Publication Data:

Wheatley, Robert, 1947-.
Railway portraits.

ISBN 0 9752450 6 6.

1. Steam-engines - New South Wales - Pictorial works. 2.
Railroads - New South Wales - Pictorial works. I. Wheatley,
Bruce, 1950-. II. Title.

385.36109944

Journeys end. 3822 and 3820, Newcastle – May 1970.

Foreword

I think it's the *smell*. The smell is produced by the impregnating of the steam with oil in order to lubricate the cylinders; it's sort of semi-vaporised. It's a peculiar smell of hot oil (which it is). Then there's the smell of *coal*, something one does not experience much nowadays because of all the modern houses with their non-Santa-friendly-chimney-less constructions. So, I put the smell of these mobile kettles as their first appeal.

Next, the *sound*. Oh, what an invention! How could something so big and noisy, and sweet smelling also be so useful? What a conjoining of good things! What a rarity. What a great pity they are all but gone. Why?

These locomotives (even the name is really quaint) are generally appealing to men. I remember my confusion when my mother said "we'd better go now" only *minutes* after I left a recently stationary train at Central at Sydney. After a wonderful trip down the mountains, I had run down to the puffing engine at the front to stand in absolute entertainment at this wonderful beast. She said we "should go" after only a few *minutes*? How could anything else that the day had to offer compete with this marvellous toy? Our relationship was never quite the same again.

To *drive* a big train with a big steam engine at the front is bliss upon bliss. I have done it. Despite the engine's appearance, it has to be treated well. One would release the brakes, watch the gauges to make sure all the pipes were charged, then pull the regulator out, and then push it back in, so that the important initial momentum would be encouraged. I was a good driver (when some benevolent, sooty man gave me the opportunity), and it was the mark of a good driver (*inter alia*) to get up to speed without spinning the wheels.

And not all engines were the same. On paper, and in the workshop, you'd say they were identical, but out on the road, there were often many subtle differences, and very evident on those big hills. The whistle and safety valves were there to drown out the swearing.

I miss the steam locomotive a *lot*.

Pictures of them are like some vague, distant cousin. But, they're better than no relatives at all.

Enjoy this book in front of a coal fire… if you can find one.

Clive Robertson,
TV & Radio Presenter, Sydney.

3

First light. 3617, Mittagong – July 1967.

The steam locomotive was an experience of the senses which had few equals in the mechanical world. It inspired artists, poets, writers and musicians. This machine was designed as a workhorse, but its qualities quickly transformed it into an object of fascination. It captivated generations and its image is buried deep into human consciousness.

Argyle Street. 3638+5902, Moss Vale – May 1969.

Introduction

The romance of railways died with the passing of the steam locomotive. It was an undeniably beautiful creature that captivated and inspired generations, its image a potent reminder of the days when fire and steam was the heart of railway operation.

Sentimentality, however, is no match for economics and the inefficiency of the steam locomotive made its demise inevitable. Replacing steam with diesels dislocated whole communities and skills honed over generations became superfluous overnight. The men who maintained, drove and fired these locomotives worked in a fusion of coal, flame, grease and steam. It was a world of physical exertion, shift work and mateship. Capturing this life and the essence of the steam locomotive was our passion. *Railway Portraits* records the atmosphere of a steam railway before modern traction sterilised its operation. Photographs cover the years 1964 to 1979 and include special train workings that occurred after regular steam had finished.

Our photographic style was greatly influenced by the work of British railway photographer Colin T. Gifford. The challenge was to capture the steam locomotive's relationship with landscape, topography, railway staff and the public. Tolstoy wrote, "The aim of the artist ... is to make people love life in all its countless inexhaustible manifestations." If our photographic perspective prompts these feelings then our task has been achieved.

Robert & Bruce Wheatley
Sydney, 2006.

Steam's Slow Demise

The depression and WW2 left the NSW railways rundown and in desperate need of new investment. As part of the modernisation program the first mainline diesel-electric entered service in 1951. Given the economic advantages of this new form of motive power the decision was made in the mid 1950s to completely dieselise the system, accompanied by bold predictions of steam's demise in the early 1960s.

Dieselisation of the North Coast in 1960 and electrification to Lithgow (1957) and Gosford (1960) made large inroads into steam stocks. With continuing influx of diesels, by the early 1960s large portions of the south, far west and north west of the state had fallen, and steam became an endangered species.

Steam's steady decline was slowed following a bumper grain harvest in 1963/64. But with dieselisation of the Illawarra line, Riverina Express and southern mail trains in 1964 and the reduction in goods traffic following the drought of 1965, steam's future looked bleak.

Another large harvest late in 1966 saw many steam locomotives retrieved from storage roads, and 1967 would be its last big year. Steam returned to Werris Creek, and was in widespread use in the Cowra and Dubbo districts moving the golden grain. However the reprieve was temporary and by years end these workings had ceased.

The Department's plan for complete dieselisation was impeded by lack of finance, increasing traffic and to add salt to the wound, the failure of older diesels. So drastic was the motive power shortage that the decision was made late in 1968 to return steam to the long dieselised North Coast line to Taree and extend steam workings to Murrurundi on the Main North. These forays lasted into 1969. This year saw steam operation to Goulburn cease and its presence around Sydney metropolitan area greatly reduced.

Steam was retained for yard shunting, local trip working and some banking duties in many locations around the state, but even in this diminished role its days were numbered.

The last remaining steam stronghold centred on coal rich Newcastle, with workings to Gosford and the lower Hunter Valley lasting several more years. 1970 saw the last working of 38 class in regular service including their use on the Newcastle Expresses. The last regular steam hauled passenger train in Australia, the Newcastle-Singleton service came to an end in July 1971.

The close of 1972 saw steam finish out of Broadmeadow and Port Waratah depots, and for all intents and purposes the system was fully dieselised. As if the era of the steam locomotive refused to die, a lone warrior, garratt 6042 battled on till February 1973, being the last steam locomotive in regular government railway service in Australia.

The process of dieselisation lasted more than 20 years, which delighted railway enthusiasts but was a constant source of frustration for the Department. The state now had a dieselised railway, however much track, signalling and rolling stock belonged to the 1920s era, the last period in which major capital investment was undertaken.

Newcastle Flyer. Tickhole tunnel, Kotara – September 1965.

The 38 class, introduced between 1943 and 1949, were the pride of the railways. The first five of 30 locomotives were streamlined and featured a bullet nose with a central headlight. Their superb high-speed performance and cracking exhaust were legendary, and the design so successful they outperformed the diesels of the era on passenger work.

The class retained its prowess well into the 1960s and were still found working passenger trains like the Newcastle Express as late as 1970.

Destination board. Central concourse – March 1971.

The destination board at Sydney's Central Station was a prominent feature of the main concourse. This 1906 masterpiece was operated via an ingenious ground level mechanism, enabling staff to change station names, platforms and times. For many Sydneysiders, the expression "meet me under the clock" needed no further explanation.

Campbelltown train. 3219, Burwood – December 1965.

The 32 class were a very successful design. One hundred and ninety one of these locomotives were delivered between 1892 and 1911. Although designed for express passenger work, they performed equally well on all manner of traffic throughout NSW. So outstanding was this class that all remained in service until 1956. It's remarkable that this 73-year-old locomotive was still hauling passenger trains from Sydney terminal in 1965.

Lithgow bound. 3626, Wallerawang – January 1966.

A work stained 36 class drifts through Wallerawang on No.364 goods. The train has only a few miles to travel before entering electrified territory and a change of motive power to conquer the Blue Mountains. The white stain covering the boiler and cylinders is the residue of impurities boiled out of hard western water.

Coonamble Mail. 3639+3648, Dubbo – November 1965.

The 36 class were delivered between 1925 and 1928, and rebuilt in the mid 1950s. They were regarded by many as a typical, rugged-looking Australian locomotive and are seen here departing Dubbo. It was common practice to 'double head' many Sydney-bound mail trains from Dubbo as numerous 1-in-40 grades were encountered between Wellington and Orange.

Thunder in the hills. 5369+6028, Hawkmount – December 1967.

Beneath a canopy of coal smoke, the zinc concentrate train from Broken Hill nears the end of its journey to Sulphide Junction. The volcanic exhaust from the mechanically-stoked garratt dwarfs the plume from the leading hand-fired loco.

The 60 class were a Garratt design and placed in service between 1952 and 1957. Garratts comprised three frames which were pivoted, allowing the locomotive to negotiate track curvature. The front engine unit contained a water tank, the middle unit the cab and boiler, while the rear engine unit contained another water tank and coal bunker.

Under a blackened thundercloud of its own making, a bunker-first garratt heads south with a load of northern coal. In steam days, fettlers cleared trackside vegetation to minimise the risk of fire from burning cinders. Their accommodation was often under canvas and a tent frame remains on the embankment.

Hauling 'black gold'. 6018, Fassifern – September 1967.

Focused on every exhaust beat, the driver of No.619 goods listens for any hint of wheel slip as he coaxes the heavy train up the grade. In the steam era, schoolboys dreamed of being engine drivers. To them these men in overalls were heroes.

Cresting Hawkmount. 6037 – August 1968.

Night crossing. 3651+5905 refuged, 5910 Up main, Bargo – January 1969.

Night time hides the detail of day and heightens the senses. Under the cloak of darkness, the mystique of the steam locomotive is enhanced. The fires' vivid orange glow illuminated the crew labouring in the cab and cast wild flickering patterns on escaping steam.

No.31 South. 3825, Campbelltown – February 1967.

For many years Gosford was the limit of electrification from Sydney and was the changeover point for motive power. It was the stage where many a grand performance was played out as trains were relayed north under a banner of smoke and steam. The changing of the guard would see the efficient electric locomotive uncouple and slip away, then from the yard, billowing clouds of steam would erupt as a primeval form of locomotion emerged to couple to the train.

A double headed north bound goods waits for the passage of the Newcastle paper train. The lights of the electric loco that hauled the train from Sydney can be seen in the glistening maze of track. The fireman of the lead engine had earlier questioned whether night photography was possible so it's not surprising he watched amused as this early morning scene was recorded.

Changing of the guard. 5906+6009 and 3818, Gosford – November 1966.

King of the road. 3813, Newcastle Express, Gosford – April 1970.

Green-liveried 3813 stands majestically at the head of the evening Newcastle Express. A pillar of steam roars from open safety valves and the air compressor pumps with a lusty chant, her motion cloaked in a veil of steam.

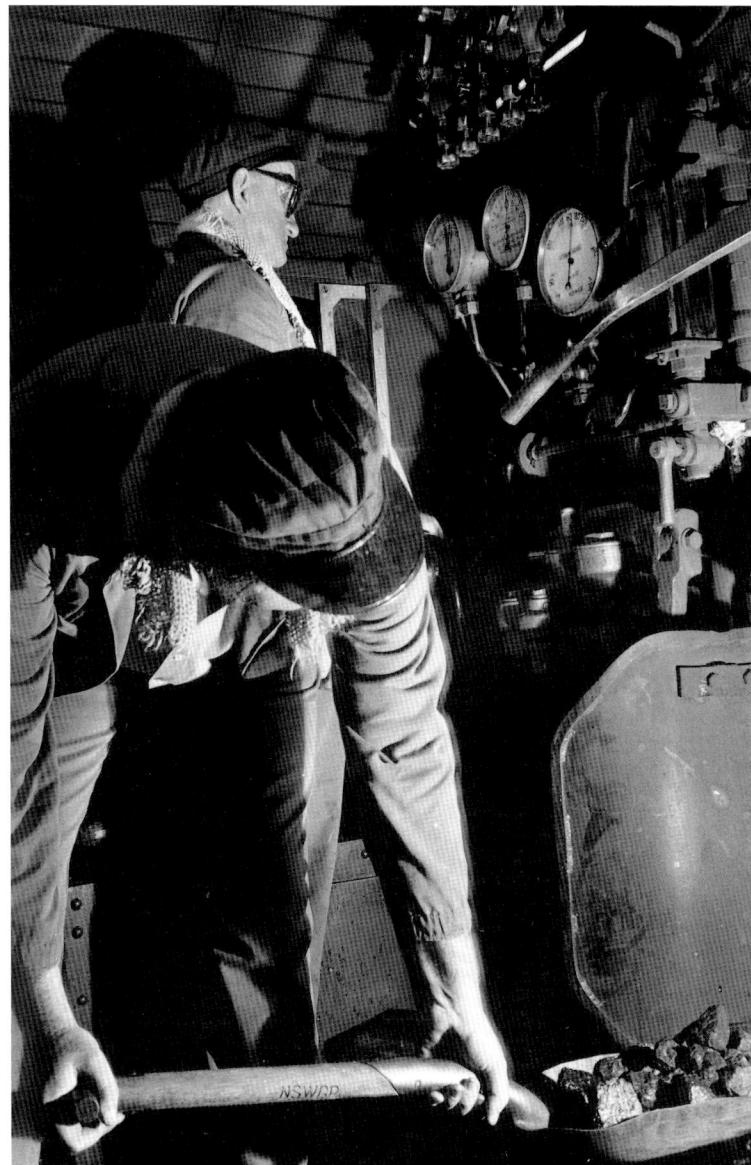

Teamwork. 3526, Murrurundi – May 1971.

The steam engine was often temperamental, demanding the skilled efforts and teamwork of the crew to control the untamed forces of burning coal, boiling water and high pressure steam. A loco's performance was only as good as its crew. With steam's demise, the inseparable relationship between driver, fireman and locomotive was broken as modern power was largely automated.

Night shift. 5407, Hexham – May 1972.

Ready for the road. Moss Vale – December 1966.

Steam wafting through a flame-lit cab, whirring turbo, the smell of hot cylinder oil and the aroma of coal smoke fill the air as 3820 prepares for the road ahead on No. 329 south. Positioning the locomotive cab opposite the round metal marker plate ensured the tender was in the correct alignment for the water column.

Coaling. 3024, Enfield – July 1968.

Coal stage. 6042, Broadmeadow – September 1972.

Coal stages were massive timber structures used for coaling and sanding locomotives and were a prominent feature of many railway towns. The fuelman's view from the stage was of gaping tenders shrouded in steam and clouds of dust from coal cascading down chutes into bunkers.

Backplate. 3214, Junee – March 1978.

Sunrise. 5278, Port Waratah – August 1968.

Headlight cleaning. 3246, Broadmeadow – September 1970.

Fitter. Port Waratah – August 1968.

Driver Tony McClosky. Darling Harbour – September 1969.

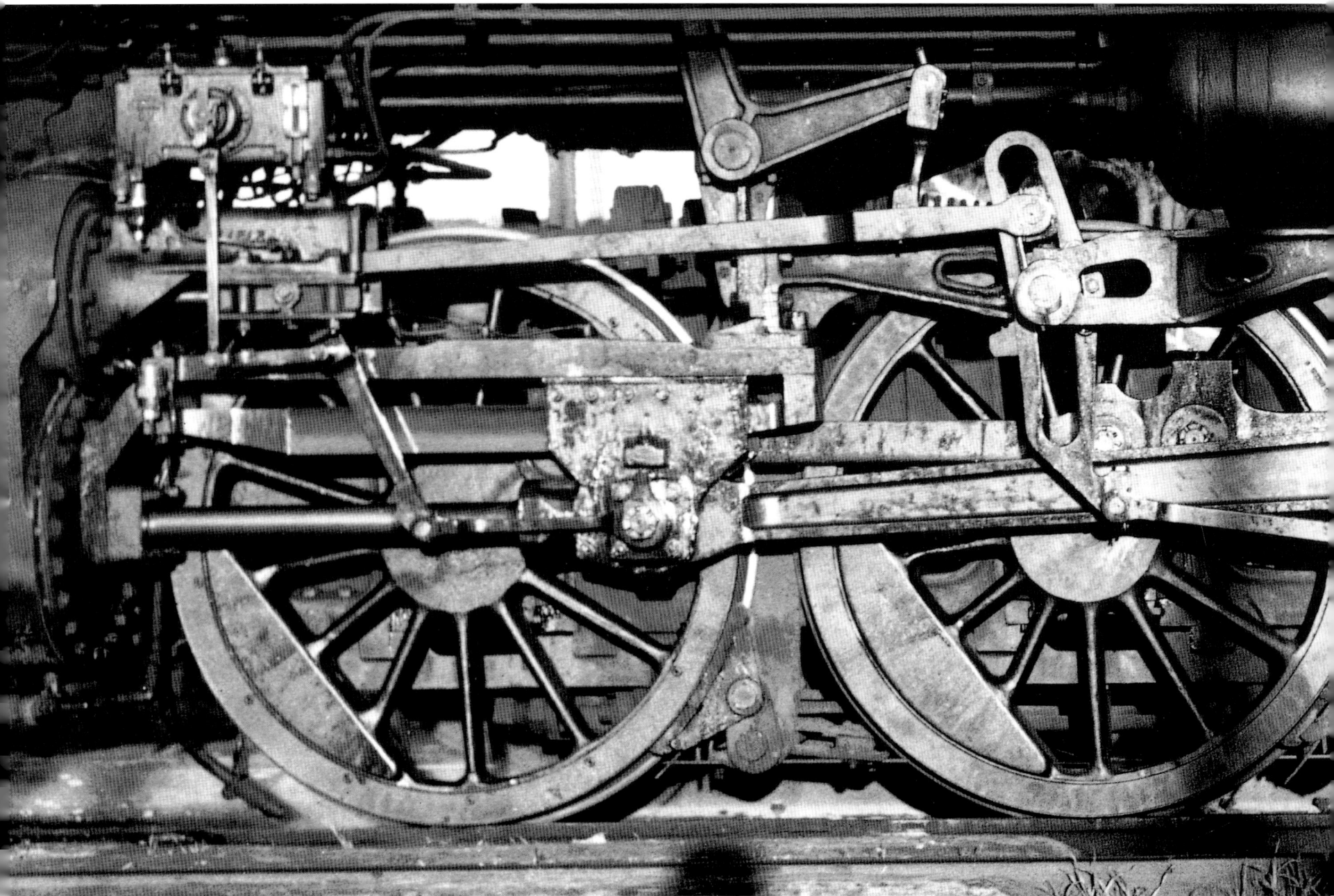

Wheels and rods. 5910, Moss Vale – April 1969.

"Viscount's Australians". 6042, Ravensworth – October 1972.

"We smoke for taste". 3214, Picton – November 1976.

Riverstone pub. 3028T – December 1970.

A scene framed in the mind's eye can be ruined when an unforeseen circumstance arises. All was well until this larrikin jumped to his feet yelling, "Hey, take my photo!". Cursing turned to delight as the photograph was taken to accommodate his intrusion.

Fuelman. Vic Rivett, Tarana – September 1965.

Most east bound, steam hauled goods trains stopped at Tarana to have the loco's fire cleaned prior to climbing the western slopes of the Great Divide. Following the departure of an Up goods, Tarana's fuelman, Victor Rivett (1904–89), shovels ash from the pit. The contents of the hopper were tipped at the end of the makeshift narrow gauge track.

Kelvin "Kiwi" Haughton. 3803, Moss Vale – January 1968.

On arrival at Moss Vale, steam locomotives had battled miles of 1-in-75 gradient of the Southern Highlands. Locomotives were watered, had their fire cleaned and coal shovelled forward in the tender. Fuelman were employed in many locations to perform these essential duties. It was a grimy, unglamourous job, but one crucial to the running of a steam railway.

Men like "Kiwi" Haughton were flattered to be photographed as they were not often the subject of railway photographers.

Morning crossing. 3808 and 5056, Maldon – September 1967.

The Moss Vale train comes to a stand at Maldon as the Thirlmere goods wends it way south leaving a steam trail hanging in the crisp morning air. On cold and still winter mornings a long sinuous plume of steam would hang in the valleys and hills after the passage of a train. It was part of the romance of steam.

Rounding the curve. 3808, Picton tunnel – September 1967.

Vapour from steam-heated cars blows back along the Moss Vale train as it winds downhill into Picton. Heating carriages with locomotive steam was once common practice for trains traversing the colder regions of NSW in winter. By 1967 this service was the last in the state to use this form of heating.

Steam to spare. 3824, Picton – September 1966.

With steam rocketing from safety valves, this Eveleigh-built 4-6-2 rolls downhill, crashing over pointwork and into a fog-shrouded Picton on the Moss Vale passenger.

Midday Flyer. 3828, Fassifern – January 1966.

The station assistant waits to collect tickets from passengers as the midday Newcastle Express arrives at Fassifern. Casual dress was the order of the day; his hat the only indication he was a railway employee.

Many country platforms were short and couldn't accommodate the whole train. The last steam hauled Southern Highlands Express has been brought to a stand so the van was opposite the parcels.

Loading parcels. 3801, Yerrinbool – October 1969.

Buffer to buffer. 5461, Buxton – September 1976.

The fireman lifts the coupler in anticipation of the engine easing up to compress the buffers, enabling the link to be dropped into the hook drawgear. In the late steam era the majority of goods vehicles had been fitted with automatic couplers, however many passenger vehicles still retained hook-and-link drawgear. Automatic couplers made the job safer and did away with the lifting of heavy linkages and the necessity of buffers.

Cleaning the ashpan. 3803, Moss Vale – January 1968.

Modern steam locomotives were fitted with ashpans that could be cleaned at track level, unlike many older designs which required cleaning from underneath the engine. Water hoses were installed at de-ashing pits to aid the cleaning process. The hose is manhandled by driver Bill Carey to ensure the pan is free of ash and clinker before the train proceeds to Goulburn.

Boxpok wheels. 3803, Moss Vale – December 1967.

Overflow. 6039, Singleton – August 1968.

In Chinese Taoist philosophy, the movement of water either descending as rain or ascending as mist symbolised the interpenetration of earth with the life of heaven. What would a Taoist make of this scene, as 6031 works uphill through Kotara? Long before this spectacle unfolded, a thunderous noise boomed from the white void. First sighting was not of the locomotive, but of steam billowing in sunlit splendour above the mist. Later, the black form of the juggernaut emerged.

Emerging from the fog. 6031, Kotara – May 1967.

Hunter Valley coal. 6008, Nundah – August 1967.

The picturesque Hunter Valley, renowned for its vineyards, holds another older prize – coal. Nestled in this valley lay the Newdell Colliery. Garratt locomotives worked round the clock between the mine and seaboard loaders toting long rakes of four wheel, sixteen ton capacity wagons.

Misty morning. 3077, Robertson – February 1967.

The cross country line between Unanderra and Moss Vale was one of the early lines to be dieselised due to the steep 1-in-30 grades on the Illawarra escarpment. However, the passenger service linking Wollongong and Moss Vale remained steam hauled.

On one of the last steam workings on this service, tank locomotive 3077 gallops into Robertson with the morning passenger to Wollongong. The pure white steam trail condensing in the mountain air is replaced by coal smoke as the fireman puts fresh coal on the fire.

Greasy work. 3636, Forbes Mail, Lithgow – January 1966.

Eveleigh driver, Cyril Jackson, wipes his hands on a sweat cloth after wash-up. The cake of soap placed under the seat was often 'Lux' brand and used for its liberal foaming qualities in hard water. It was advertised as "the soap of film stars". Jokes were exchanged as crews likened themselves to pampered Hollywood stars, a far cry from the sweaty, greasy environment in which they worked.

On time arrival. 3636, Forbes Mail, Wallerawang – January 1966.

At Wallerawang the fob watch is checked to ensure he is running to the timetable. The use of such watches by railway staff was common place at the time.

Twilight reflections. 3529, Gosford – January 1967.

Kosciusko Snow Express. Strathfield – September 1966.

The Kosciusko Snow Express was a weekend, steam-heated train that operated in the colder months. Most of its passengers were destined for Cooma and the snowfields beyond. 3823 pauses at Strathfield on one of the last steam hauled workings of this service. The loco is destined for Goulburn where 32 class would then relay the express to Cooma. Many passengers on the train partied all night, oblivious to the crew in the open cab, enduring the numbing cold. Such was the lot of railwaymen.

Campbelltown service. 3320, Strathfield – June 1966.

Weekday passengers from Campbelltown were provided with a through service to Sydney terminal. These morning and evening peak hour trains were stabled at Campbelltown overnight and hauled by the reliable 32 class. The locomotives hauling these services were fitted with original six-wheel tenders to enable turning on the town's 50-foot turntable. Such workings lasted until May 1968 when electrification was extended from Liverpool.

Large Erecting Shop. 3227, 3614, Eveleigh – 1964.

The Eveleigh workshops constructed and maintained steam locomotives and carriages for the vast New South Wales system. The thousands employed here possessed specialist skills and their engineering work was a source of both railway and state pride.

Cylinder repairs. 3820, Enfield – March 1973.

With piston and cross head removed, fitter Harry Riches and his mate undertake cylinder repairs. Harry is wearing a hat folded from newspaper. This headwear was commonly used as it was light weight, comfortable and disposable at the end of the shift.

Overhaul. 3665 and 3643, Bathurst shed – August 1966.

With its driving wheels removed and resting on massive jacks, repairs are undertaken to the smokebox, cylinders and axle boxes of 3665. Servicing performed at county depots added another layer of men to the payroll and aided the town's prosperity.

Walschaert's valve gear. 3638, Mittagong – August 1968.

Loose shunting. 3229, Goulburn yard – August 1971.

In railway yards around NSW, loose shunting was common place. This was a practice where wagons were propelled by the shunting engine and freewheeled into position to form a new train. Goulburn's steam shunter, punching volleys of steam into the cold morning air, sends the end truck on its way.

Sunrise shunt. 3112, Bathurst yard – September 1971.

At Bathurst, smoke from the shunting engine and depot drift across the surrounding area, adding more soot to the town. The first light of day often found many railway towns engulfed in a thick blanket of mist and coal smoke. Smoke from steam locomotives staining washing on clothes lines was the bane of many trackside residents.

Transport of parcels was a major activity for the railways. Parcels and tarpaulin ropes are loaded onto the brakevan of the Harden mixed as the yard shunter takes water from the station column.

Station life. 3092T shunter, Cowra – February 1966.

Shunting occurred around the clock in major yards as trains were remarshalled. The outstretched arms of the shunters, (Bob Cunningham on right), indicate to the driver of the locomotive to cease pushing the wagons.

Shunting. 5274, Goulburn – February 1971.

Afternoon arrivals. 3643, Tarana – September 1965.

During the afternoon shift at Tarana, a 36 class clumps into the station on a westbound goods while on the Up, the Oberon mixed awaits departure. Smoke from the brakevan indicates the guard has his fuel heater in operation.

A mixed was a train which included both passenger and goods carriages. The passenger car was marshalled at the rear of the train next to the brakevan and was often used for the conveyance of school children and passengers connecting to main line services.

Moss Vale train. Central – October 1969.

The two faces of steam. The fireman near the end of his shift goes wearily about his task, while on the platform, passers by admire the locomotive.

Driver and guard. Cootamundra – February 1971.

First sighting. 3246, Kentucky – May 1971.

Bargo Brownies.
3638+3652, Bargo –
March 1969.

A special visit to the locomotive depot was arranged for Goulburn's primary school students. Ears are covered to suppress the deafening roar of steam as the loco eases onto the turntable.

In the lair. 3813, Goulburn roundhouse – August 1970.

The steam locomotive could be unpredictable. When at close quarters, the unsuspecting public would step back in fright as steam erupted without warning. A father photographing his children holds one child while the other recoils from an unexpected burst of steam.

Caught by surprise. 6042, Gosford loco – August 1972.

To some, their earliest recollection of a steam engine is one of fear. Perhaps it was the terror experienced when thrust into the threatening environment of the cab by a well-meaning parent, or the shock as a locomotive burst past at speed. Fear was a key to their attraction.

Awe struck. 6042, Blayney – July 1978.

Single line working over much of NSW necessitated a foolproof system to ensure only one train was in a section at any time. A metal staff was removed from the staff instrument at the signal box and strapped into a leather pouch with a cane hoop for handing to a crew member of the train about to proceed into the next section. Possession of the staff guaranteed sole occupancy of the section. Signalman related frightening experiences of drivers exceeding the safe speed when transferring staffs. Misjudged exchanges would sometimes result in the staff being lost and frantic efforts followed, particularly at night, to ensure its retrieval.

The driver leans from the cab with the staff in his gloved hand ready for the exchange with Tumulla's signalman. No stress with this transfer as the loco was down to walking pace as it hauled its tonnage up the steep grade.

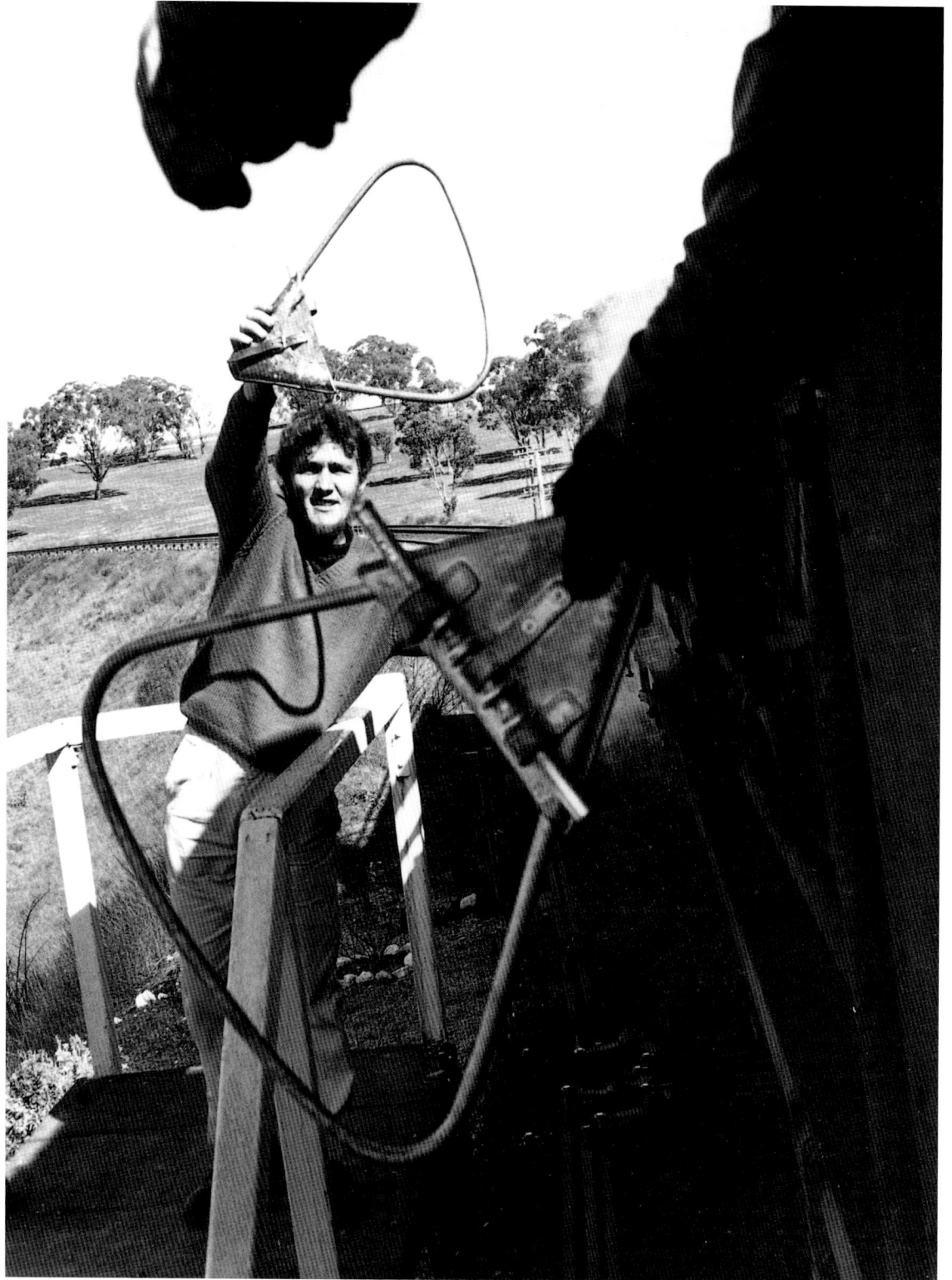

Staff exchange. 6014, Tumulla – August 1966.

A driver's view of the road ahead. Assistant engine 3649 with its turret tender leads garratt 6011 into a curve on the steeply graded climb between Molong and Orange. The articulation of the garratt's frame negotiating the curve is evidenced by the differing angle of the boiler handrail to that on the front tank.

The road ahead. 3649+6011, Molong – March 1967.

Heart of fire. 3820, Bathurst – January 1974.

An invitation into the cab of a steam locomotive was an unforgettable experience. Flaming coals and heat from the firebox, the thump of the air compressor, the smell of oil and coal smoke were intoxicating to the senses.

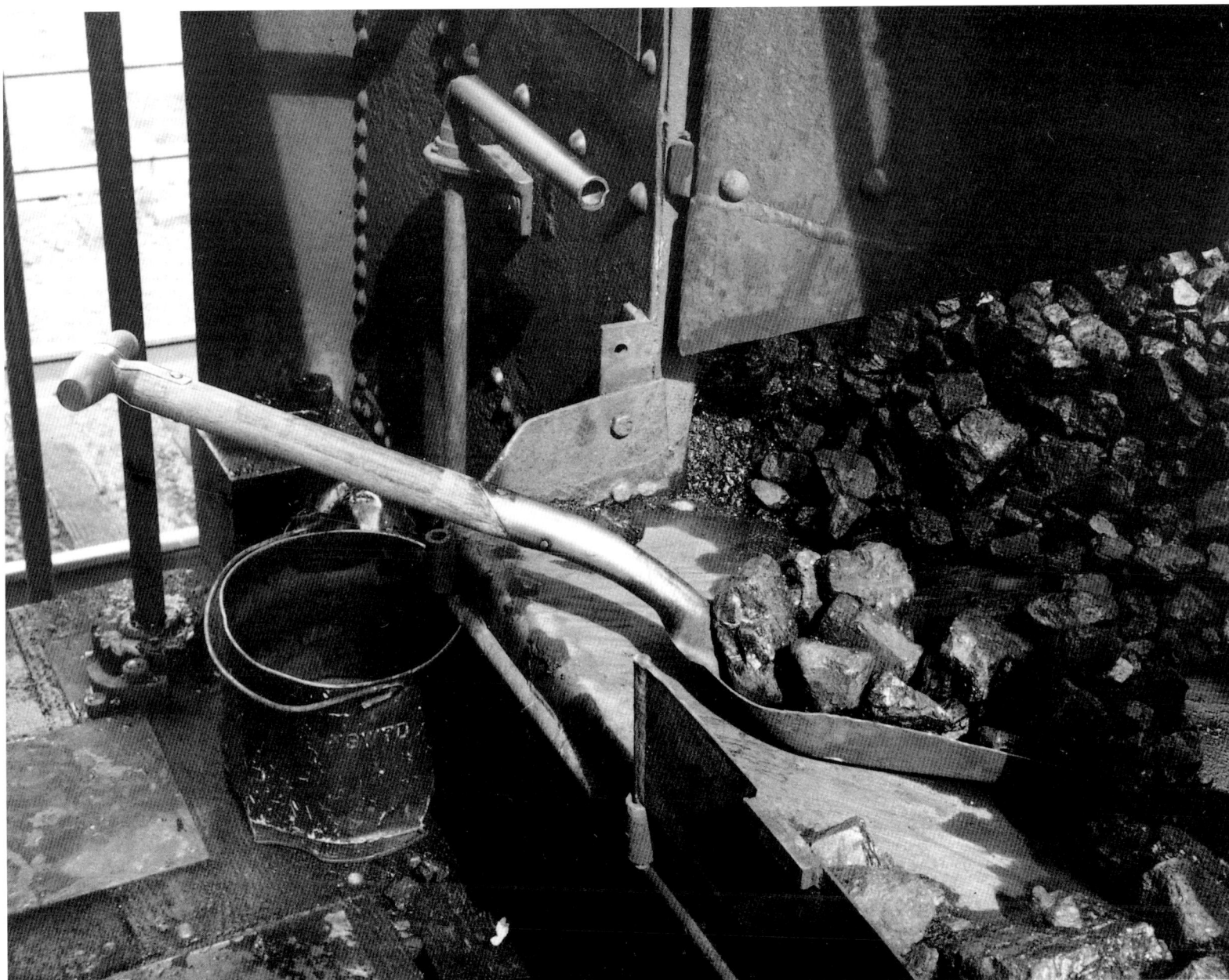

Shovel on shovel plate. 3638, Mittagong – August 1968.

The fireman's shovel was narrow and had a short handle to facilitate swinging in the confines of the cab and to allow entry through the firebox door. On the road, the fireman regularly hosed the coal to prevent dust swirling into the cab. The glistening coal and a wet cab floor indicate a recent dousing.

Wet night. 3664, Moss Vale – December 1966.

No.337 south has been placed in the refuge on this wet summer evening to allow the passage of a diesel hauled goods on the main. Two water columns were provided in many locations where double heading was common.

Waylaid. 3820, Moss Vale – September 1966.

Displaced passenger locomotives were kept in service by hauling goods trains. In times past, this locomotive would have paused only briefly at Moss Vale, working trains like the Melbourne Express. But now, in its waning years, it has time to cool its heels in the loop as diesels pass by on rosters it once held.

Proud veteran. 3374, Blayney – November 1966.

Steam locos were fitted with steam-driven turbo generators which provided electricity for the cab, marker and headlights. The loco's generator blows exhaust steam over the platform, its contented whine and the gentle hiss of steam are the only sounds to be heard in the still of the night. Behind 3374, on No.155 goods, are empty livestock wagons returning to Cowra for another consignment. On the adjacent road, sheep from Eugowra are Sydney bound on No.242 goods hauled by 3642.

Tenterfield goods. 5919, Guyra – May 1966.

The turbo generator on this locomotive had failed and kerosene marker lamps were substituted – a defect that prohibited a locos use on a passenger service.

Kerosene tail lamp. Wollongong.

One of the delights of travelling behind steam was to peer through the carriage door onto the bouncing tender while listening to the roar of the engine. On this early morning service, steam swirls over the tender and flits away. Sprays of water settle on the window as chains swing with the movement of the carriage.

Flurried steam. 3322, Richmond train – September 1966.

Smoke-filled carriages, soot-covered seating and cinders in the eye, were part of rail travel in the steam era. Passengers could endure sweltering heat by day and freezing conditions at night.

Wash basin. TAM sleeper.

Carriage compartment.

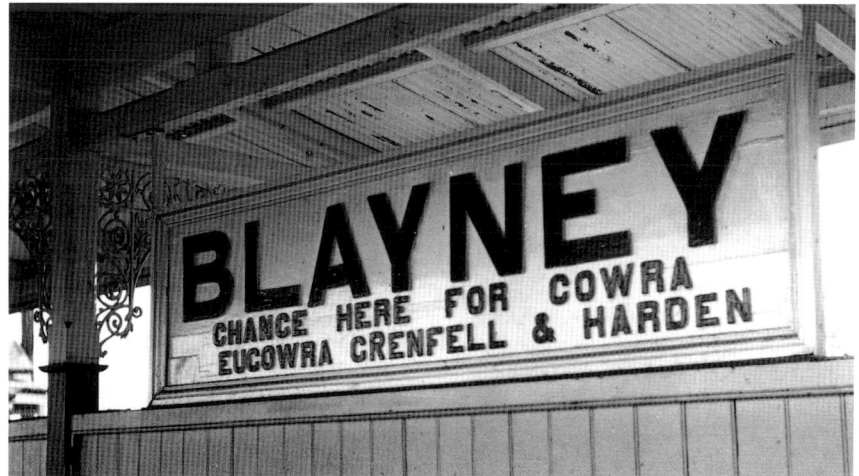

Embossed metal wash basins were found in sleeping compartments. To save space, they were hinged to the wall and lowered when in use. Upon retraction, the contents were funnelled on to the track below.

Nameboard. Blayney – July 1978.

Descending the Highlands. 3830, Exeter – August 1967.

Stonequarry Creek Viaduct. 3137, Picton – April 1979.

Winter afternoon. 6042, Carcoar – July 1978.

Rail reflection. 6042, Cowra – July 1978.

Ribbon of steel. 3203, Thirlmere - September 1976.

Homeward bound. 3827, Newbridge – November 1969.

Slaking the thirst. 3531, Singleton – February 1968.

Branch line goods. 3142T, Denman – August 1969.

Grain from Merriwa. 5278, Sandy Hollow-Denman – August 1969.

Harden Mixed. 5595, Cowra – February 1966.

West bound goods. 3675, Blayney – January 1966.

Safeworking. 3526, Woolbrook – May 1971.

Railway Clock. Harden South Box – August 1978.

Railways ran to the clock. Seth Thomas regulators were a reliable clockwork timepiece found mounted on the wall of many a signal box and office. Their reassuring ticking was often the only sound heard in the quiet periods between trains.

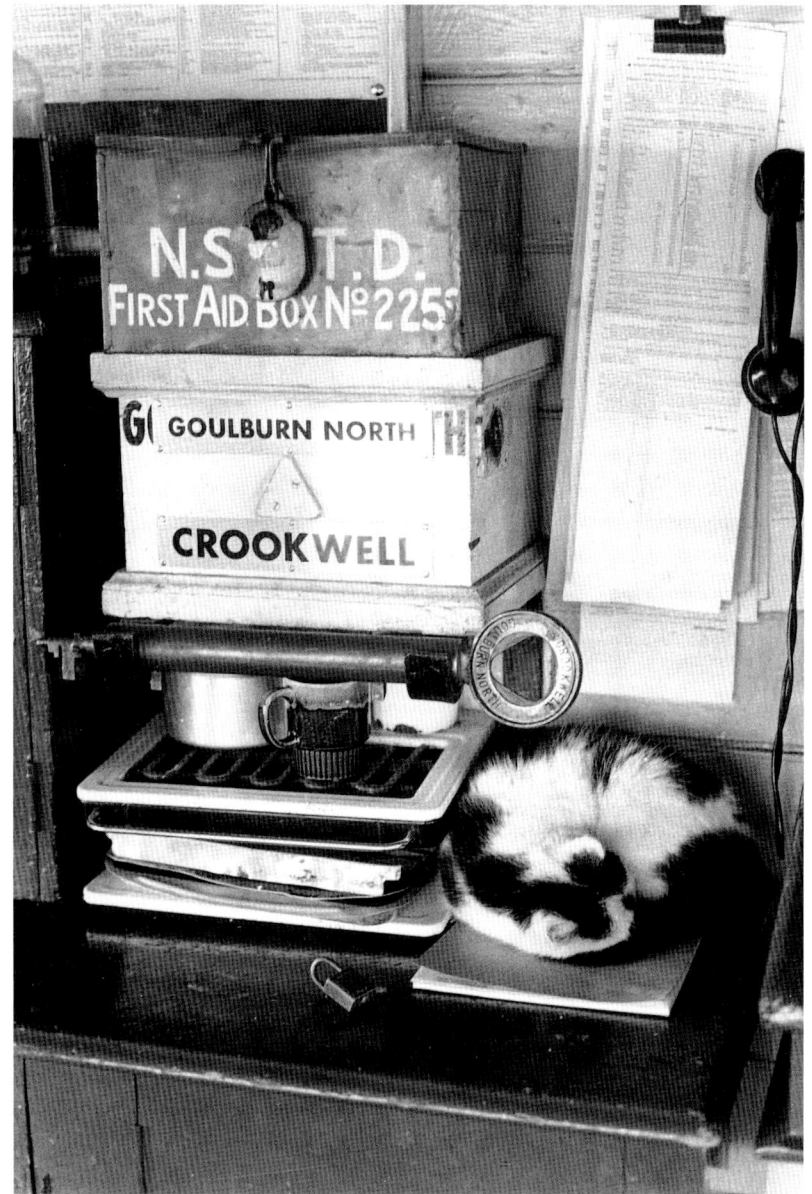
Signal box cat. Goulburn North Box – July 1978.

Refuged. 5910, Wyee – September 1972.

Harden South Box – August 1978.

Fettlers. Muswellbrook – March 1969.

Fettlers are interrupted by yard shunter 5433 making up the Merriwa goods and the passage of diesel electric 4301 working through on a north bound stock train. A garratt and a 30T class wait in the yard for their respective tonnage.

On an oppressively hot humid day at Newdell Colliery, 6023 crawls up the yard with its loaded coal hoppers in tow. The fireman, with his back to the camera, has escaped the heat of the cab during loading operations and passes the time of day with the shunters. Soon he will rejoin the loco to work the train to the docks at Port Waratah.

Heat and humidity. 6023, Newdell – October 1969.

No.631 north. 3820+6023, Hawkmount – November 1970.

The fireman's view of double garratts climbing Fassifern Bank. Within 6029's cab the mechanical stoker grinds as coal is flung into the raging firebox and a cacophony of sound assaults the senses. The tell-tale plume of saturated steam rising from 6022 indicates the loco is priming from an overfilled boiler. The track is carpeted with steam from open cocks as water-laden steam is drained to prevent damage to the cylinders.

Climbing Fassifern Bank. 6022+6029 – September 1970.

Lonely vigil. 3654, Gosford loco – December 1968.

Stabled engines. 5139, 3026T, 5476 Lithgow roundhouse – April 1971.

Awaiting their call. 3815, 3641+6019, Gosford loco – May 1967.

De-ashing. 5407, Port Waratah loco – July 1972.

Standing in the pit under the loco, clinker and ash are raked from the ashpan.

Bourke bound. 3282, Dubbo – January 1967.

3282 awaits departure from Dubbo on No.65 Bourke goods. Ahead lay 226 miles of mostly flat, semi-arid country. Along the way the train will traverse 116 miles of straight track between Nyngan and its destination Bourke, an old port town on the Darling River. Westbound trains had to negotiate a 1-in-60 grade known as Bourke Hill situated just west of Dubbo, and some goods trains were provided with rear-end assistance to climb this grade. Push up engine 3313 can be seen in the background ready to act as banker for No.65.

Evening departure. 3628+ 3811, Through Mail, Dubbo – January 1967.

5133 receives a steam clean before being forwarded to Enfield for scrapping. The belated cleaning was no sudden change of heart to make up for years of neglect, but followed a request from the scrap metal merchant that excess grime and grease be removed to aid cutting-up operations.

Steam cleaning. 5133, Port Waratah loco – December 1972.

The injector is situated under the cab, and is an appliance which uses the loco's steam to transfer water from the tender into the boiler.

After the fire was dropped on a steam engine, it continued to breathe until all the steam was drained from the boiler.

Injector steam. 3822, Broadmeadow loco – August 1970.

Raising steam. 3664, Broadmeadow - May 1967.

It took many hours to raise steam in a locomotive boiler from cold to maximum pressure. The time and labour involved was one of steams drawbacks.

Pungent coal smoke oozing from the opened smokebox door fills the roundhouse as 3664 is prepared for working an evening mail train from Broadmeadow.

The mighty 57 and 58 class 4-8-2s were early casualties of electrification and dieselisation. All of the 58s were withdrawn by 1957 following electrification to Lithgow, leaving the older 57s to work out their final days hauling heavy goods trains on the Illawarra and Main Southern line. The last of these 'big engines', 5711, was officially withdrawn in October 1961.

The loco was retained for preservation and resides in Enfield roundhouse, silent and cold, its working life now over.

Last of the tribe. 5711, Enfield - April 1967.

Gloomy day. 5412, 5456, 5178, 1904, 3142T Port Waratah – August 1971.

Port Waratah depot was unique, its only purpose was to provide locomotives for the haulage of black coal. Many of these coal trains consisted of non air hoppers and were limited in tonnage and speed as braking was only provided by engine and brake van. The undemanding nature of these workings allowed the use of locomotives, many of which were in poor condition, to work out their last days from this depot before overhaul or scrapping.

Ash pit. 5451, Port Waratah loco – October 1972.

Michael Hogan, weary from the night shift takes a breather. His mate, complete with breathing apparatus, shovels cinders from the smokebox into the ash pit below. Brazier and humpy afforded basic comfort. The advent of dieselisation and electrification greatly improved working conditions on the railway. While enthusiasts delighted in steam, many of those involved in its daily operation were glad to see its demise.

Water stop. 5901+5917, Gloucester – May 1969.

Mates. 5919 and 6039, Broadmeadow loco – August 1971.

Smoko. Port Waratah roundhouse – August 1971.

Port Waratah roundhouse was in a dilapidated state in its final years. Workers improvised a meal area at the back of the shed to protect themselves from the elements. Upholstered seating from a passenger carriage and a tarpaulin have been commandeered as furnishings and a flued brazier provided warmth.

Oil cans. Broadmeadow loco –
September 1972.

The overhaul of this locomotive at
Port Waratah in July 1972 may well
have been the last at this shed. The
first diesel arrived at the depot in
August 1972 and by December that
year steam had ceased.

Tone up. 5468, Port Waratah
roundhouse – July 1972.

Cleaning the smokebox. 5069, Port Waratah loco – July 1972.

This 1903 vintage loco in original condition is serviced at Port Waratah. 5069 remained in regular traffic until 22 December 1972, being the final day of steam working on the coal roads of Newcastle.

Under the yard lights. 6039+6018, Broadmeadow – September 1972.

By September 1972 less than a dozen steam locos worked out of Broadmeadow on mainline duties. Full dieselisation was only months away. Double headed garratts stand in Broadmeadow yard after bringing a goods from Gosford. The crews were eager to end their shifts and only just enough time was available for a photograph before the engines were uncoupled.

Railway children. Riverstone – January 1969.

Friendly wave. 6023, 44 class, Newdell – October 1969.

At the buffer stop. 3811, Central – October 1969.

The era of the mini-skirt coincided with the last years of steam locomotion. In October 1969, regular steam hauled passenger trains into Central had almost finished, and for many of these passengers it would be the last time they travelled behind steam.

Power and speed. Newcastle Express, Fassifern – September 1967.

Beneath a textbook trail of coal smoke, 3809 powers the morning Newcastle Express through Fassifern. At the controls was Con Cardew, the former Assistant Chief Mechanical Engineer of the NSWGR, who had a reputation for extracting the best performance out of a loco. Even in retirement Con's authority was unchallenged, his arrival on the footplate, often unannounced, would see the driver relinquish control.

Leaning from the cab, Con exchanges greetings with fellow enthusiasts. Smoking brake shoes attempt to slow the progress of this 195-ton thoroughbred as it passes in a blur of flashing rods and wheels.

Morning departure. 5901+5917, Bundook – May 1969.

End of the era. 6042, Wangi Wangi – February 1973.

Posing in front of their charge; guard Leonard Kay, driver Leonard Young and fireman Patrick Muldoon share the honour of crewing the last regular operated steam working on a government railway system in Australia. Minutes after this photograph was taken on 23 February 1973, 6042 departed Wangi with a load of empty hoppers bound for Awaba State Mine and into history.

3802, withdrawn from service in January 1967 and condemned in June that year, awaits scrapping at Cardiff workshops. Serviceable parts have been stripped from the loco to keep other 38s on the road. In August 1968 this once proud locomotive was reduced to a pile of scrap metal destined for the blast furnace.

Cannibalised. 3802, Cardiff – August 1967.

Sitting in the dirt at Sims scrap yard, 3810's driving wheels feel the heat of the oxyacetylene torch, a far cry from the days when these wheels were balanced in the workshops for 90 m.p.h. running. Opinions about the scrapping of steam locomotives varied widely. To the accountant and scrap metal dealer they were obsolescent pieces of ironmongery whose only value was monetary. To some railwaymen wearied from a hard life on the road the comment, "The only good steam engine is the one being scrapped at Sims" summed up their feelings. For enthusiasts, steam was an affair of the heart and its passing lamented.

Last remains. 3810, Mascot – May 1970.

Last exit from Enfield. 6042, 3237, 3026T – October 1974.

The decision to demolish Enfield locomotive depot to make way for a container terminal necessitated the removal of locomotives retained for preservation to other sites. Shunters from the nearby yard witness the spectacle as these engines depart Enfield for the last time.

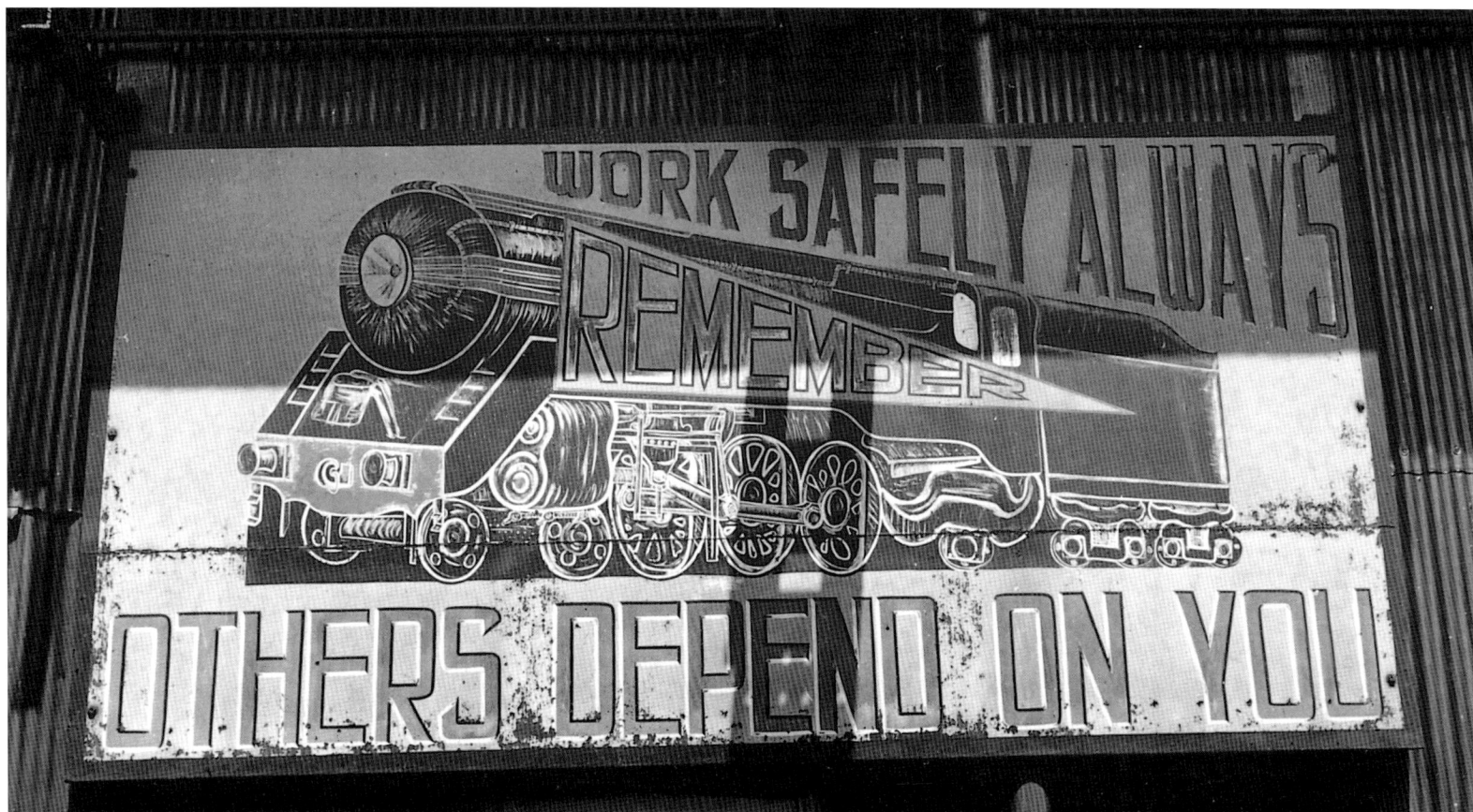

Eveleigh – 1971.

Acknowledgements

Most railway staff were friendly and accepting people. Despite the demands of their work they found time to provide information and in many cases allowed us to share their working day. Their assistance and generosity is greatly appreciated, as many photographs would not have been possible without their consent.

We are indebted to railwaymen John Simpson, Max Rivett, Graham Bennett and Colin Lewis who assisted us in identifying some of the men pictured in this book.

Gratitude to Robyn, Christina, Cameron, Natasha and Jarrod Wheatley for their contribution and support and for the encouragement of our friends John Nelson, Graham Palmer, Adrian Rynberk, Rob Turner and David Williams who shared many of our journeys.

We wish to thank Victoria Jefferys and Paul Burrows from WriteLight Pty Ltd and Clive Robertson for their valued input into *Railway Portraits*.

The following publications were used as reference material

- The *NSW Digest* magazine published by the Australian Railway Historical Society,
- *Steam Locomotive Data* published by the Public Transport Commission
- *Freight Vehicles* published by the Public Transport Commission
- *NSW Railways Curve and Gradient Diagrams*